FreeCAD [How-to]

Solid Modeling with the power of Python

Brad Collette

Daniel Falck

[PACKT] PUBLISHING

open source *
community experience distilled

BIRMINGHAM - MUMBAI

FreeCAD [How-to]

First published: September 2012

Production Reference: 1070912

Published by Packt Publishing Ltd.
Livery Place
35 Livery Street
Birmingham B3 2PB, UK.

ISBN 978-1-84951-886-4

www.packtpub.com

Credits

Authors
Brad Collette
Daniel Falck

Reviewers
Yorik van Havre
Adrian Przekwas

Acquisition Editor
Mary Jasmine Nadar

Commissioning and Content Editors
Meeta Rajani
Priyanka Shah

Technical Editor
Joyslita D'Souza

Project Coordinator
Michelle Quadros

Proofreader
Aaron Nash

Indexer
Hemangini Bari

Production Coordinator
Prachali Bhiwandkar

Cover Work
Prachali Bhiwandkar

Cover Image
Manu Joseph

Foreword

The FreeCAD project was started around 2002 by two German engineers, Jürgen Riegel and Werner Mayer. It was very ambitious. The Computer Aided Design (CAD) world was, and still is, dominated by a few high-level commercial applications that have large teams of developers behind them.

The event that made it possible to create an open source professional-grade CAD application was the open sourcing of the OpenCasCade library, a powerful 3D modeling kernel, which is a core component of FreeCAD. After that, very clever ideas about how a modern CAD application should behave and be developed helped it evolve to its present form. Although it still cannot compete with its commercial counterparts, it begins to be very useful for small CAD projects.

I discovered the project around 2006, watched it for some time, then began to write some scripts for it, and in 2008 I officially joined the development team. The community of developers, users, and enthusiasts around the project is now growing faster than ever; this helps the project to reach higher development speed and quality level, and it is thrilling to see now the first steps of FreeCAD in the professional world.

I have also known Dan Falck for a long time, from the old mailing lists, when we were all desperately looking for ways to do CAD work on the Linux platform. Dan is a well-known figure of the Linux, CAD, and CNC world, and worked a lot on HeeksCAD, a very close cousin of FreeCAD, also based on the OpenCasCade kernel. Along the road, Dan got more and more involved with FreeCAD too, contributing several additions to the FreeCAD project, and has many more ideas in the drawer.

A little bit later, from the HeeksCAD and CNC community also came the famous Brad Collette (known as Sliptonic, in the open source CADCAM world). These are two heavyweights of the open source CAD world, and no book about FreeCAD could have had better authors.

Yorik van Havre
FreeCAD developer

About the Authors

Brad Collette once designed software for a big company but doesn't like to remember that. These days, he is an entrepreneur, hobbyist, jack-of-all-trades, and a gentleman farmer. He is engaged in a multi-year project to raise two hacker sons. He has contributed to numerous open source projects and is an organizing member of Columbia Gadget Works, central Missouri's finest hackerspace.

Daniel Falck has always been interested in how things work. As a boy, he learned to play the guitar and decided to learn how to build guitars. This later progressed into learning how to make the tools that help build guitars. He still exhibits this sort of behavior today, as he tries to learn how to build open source CADCAM software that helps him build other tools of the trade, as well as guitar parts.

In the past, he has worked for Gibson Guitar Corporation as a tooling designer and prototype machine shop supervisor, where he learned CAD software. He currently does the same thing for Chris King Precision Components, running the prototype machine shop, designing tooling, gaging, fixtures, machine parts, and software.

Over the years, he has gained an appreciation for open source software and has been involved with several open source CADCAM projects. Linuxcnc was the inspiration that got him interested in Linux and open source. He has also participated in APTOS, the HeeksCNC project, and now FreeCAD.

I would like to thank the developers and users of FreeCAD, who are building a powerful open source CAD program together. Thanks go to Jürgen Riegel, Werner Mayer, and Yorik van Havre for creating such a wonderful application.

Brad and I have collaborated in the past, writing an article on HeeksCNC, for Digital Machinist Magazine. I would like to thank Brad for working with me again.

About the Reviewers

Yorik van Havre is an architect, 3D artist, and open source software enthusiast. He lives and works in Brazil, is one of the developers of the FreeCAD project, and is an active member of several other open source projects communities, such as Blender. He has reviewed several other books for Packt, including *Blender 3D Architecture, Buildings, and Scenery* and *Blender 2.5 Lighting and Rendering*. He regularly publishes articles about his work, architecture, and 3D and open source software on his site at `http://yorik.uncreated.net`.

Adrian Przekwas is a Master of Science in Mechanical Engineering. He is a design engineer in a mid-sized Polish company. The company produces steel constructions and develops solutions for the mining industry. He is an open source software and automotive technology enthusiast.

www.PacktPub.com

Support files, eBooks, discount offers and more

You might want to visit www.PacktPub.com for support files and downloads related to your book.

Did you know that Packt offers eBook versions of every book published, with PDF and ePub files available? You can upgrade to the eBook version at www.PacktPub.com and as a print book customer, you are entitled to a discount on the eBook copy. Get in touch with us at service@packtpub.com for more details.

At www.PacktPub.com, you can also read a collection of free technical articles, sign up for a range of free newsletters and receive exclusive discounts and offers on Packt books and eBooks.

http://PacktLib.PacktPub.com

Do you need instant solutions to your IT questions? PacktLib is Packt's online digital book library. Here, you can access, read and search across Packt's entire library of books.

Why Subscribe?

- ▶ Fully searchable across every book published by Packt
- ▶ Copy and paste, print and bookmark content
- ▶ On demand and accessible via web browser

Free Access for Packt account holders

If you have an account with Packt at www.PacktPub.com, you can use this to access PacktLib today and view nine entirely free books. Simply use your login credentials for immediate access.

Table of Contents

Preface

FreeCAD is a general purpose modeling tool aimed at the engineering world. Unlike other modeling tools such as Blender or Maya, which are designed for animators and artists, FreeCAD puts heavy emphasis on parametric, feature-based design.

Originally designed for Mechanical Engineering and Product Design, FreeCAD is now being developed to add functionality for a wide cross-section of engineering disciplines.

A great deal of foresight and planning has gone into the underlying technology of FreeCAD. The result is a tool that is powerful, easy to use, and easy to extend.

The pervasive use of the powerful scripting language Python is partly responsible for FreeCAD's flexibility and rapid development. End users have access to this power as well, in several different ways. From recording macros that automate simple tasks to directly creating and manipulating geometry, almost anything is possible.

Virtually every aspect of the FreeCAD application is accessible through the built-in Python interpreter. Even the user interface can be accessed and extended with Python code, permitting the user to create new dialog screens and entire modules that extend the core functionality. An example of how far this concept can be pushed is the Arch module. This workbench is being developed by Yorik van Havre to provide architectural design capabilities. It is written entirely in Python.

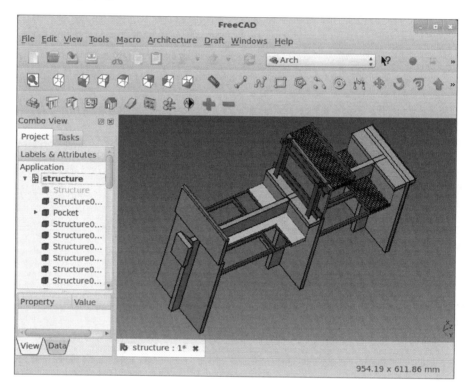

Its open architecture, extensible design, rapid development pace, and enthusiastic community make up for many of its limitations. It runs equally well on all three major platforms and has been translated into numerous languages. That, along with its free price tag, means anyone can experiment with FreeCAD now.

What this book covers

Getting and installing FreeCAD (Must know), will walk through the basics of getting FreeCAD working on your computer. Latest and greatest, or stable and easy? Mac, Windows, or Linux? We'll show you your options and talk about the trade-offs.

Understanding the FreeCAD interface (Must know), provides a broad look at FreeCAD's organization. This recipe will walk you through the user interface and get you comfortable customizing it for your own use.

CSG modeling in the Part workbench (Must know), shows you how to start with simple shapes and combine them to build complex objects. CSG modeling is one of several important techniques that FreeCAD makes possible, and an indispensable part of your modeling tool kit.

Recording and editing a macro (Should know), makes life easier by recording and playing back a sequence of frequently used commands. Create your own custom commands or automate a routine task.

Modeling a simple part with the Draft workbench (Must know), introduces another modeling technique available in FreeCAD. Many designs, even complex 3D objects, start out as 2D drawings. The Draft workbench provides tools for working with circles, arcs, lines, and other 2D elements.

Rotating and extruding to create parts (Should know), will show how 2D drawings can be turned into 3D models. Rotation and extrusion are two more tools that every FreeCAD user should know.

Creating 3D solids with Python (Become an expert), shows how to use Python to create custom 3D objects. Python is another powerful tool in your FreeCAD toolbox.

Creating a custom dialog to automate a task (Become an expert), will show you how to make your Python scripts easier to use by making a custom user interface. You can create a nice looking dialog box.

Modeling with constraints (Must know), covers one of the most powerful techniques available to the FreeCAD user. Need to change one aspect of your model without breaking the rest? Designing with constraints means building flexibility into the design. Now your designs can be easily adjusted with predictable results.

Using external constraints (Should know), will go beyond simple sketches by using some of the advanced sketching tools in FreeCAD. You can model additional features on the faces of existing objects and attach sketches to existing objects.

Adding or modifying constraints with Python (Become an expert), brings the power of Python to bear on constraint based modeling. You can dig deeper into the inner workings of sketch constraints with the Python scripting.

Creating a drawing of a part (Should know), teaches you to present your 3D design to the 2D world by creating a drawing that's ready for printing.

Exporting DXF files for other applications (Should know), will show you how to export your design to other applications using industry standard DXF files. The time will come when you need to do something with your project outside of FreeCAD and exporting is invaluable.

Importing data (Should know), will give you information on how to interact with designs made in other applications.

What you need for this book

FreeCAD is a standalone design tool. Once installed, nothing additional is needed to begin designing complex models. If you want to compile the latest version of FreeCAD, open source tools are available on the Internet, including the Git version control system necessary for downloading the source code.

Who this book is for

Written specifically for new users of CAD software with little or no experience, this book will also help users of other CAD applications get familiar with FreeCAD's unique concepts quickly.

Conventions

In this book, you will find a number of styles of text that distinguish between different kinds of information. Here are some examples of these styles, and an explanation of their meaning.

Code words in text are shown as follows: "Notice how it gives you a helpful tip on the `makeBox` class."

A block of code is set as follows:

```
import FreeCAD
import Part

App.ActiveDocument.addObject("Part::Box","Box")
FreeCAD.getDocument("Unnamed").getObject("Box").Width = 20.00
```

When we wish to draw your attention to a particular part of a code block, the relevant lines or items are set in bold:

```
QtCore.QObject.connect \
(self.okButton, QtCore.SIGNAL("pressed()"),self.box)
```

New terms and **important words** are shown in bold. Words that you see on the screen, in menus or dialog boxes for example, appear in the text like this: "Select the wire and click on the **Upgrade** button to convert it to a face."

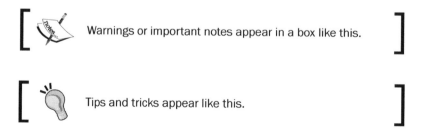

Warnings or important notes appear in a box like this.

Tips and tricks appear like this.

Reader feedback

Feedback from our readers is always welcome. Let us know what you think about this book—what you liked or may have disliked. Reader feedback is important for us to develop titles that you really get the most out of.

To send us general feedback, simply send an e-mail to feedback@packtpub.com, and mention the book title via the subject of your message.

If there is a book that you need and would like to see us publish, please send us a note in the **SUGGEST A TITLE** form on www.packtpub.com or e-mail suggest@packtpub.com.

If there is a topic that you have expertise in and you are interested in either writing or contributing to a book, see our author guide on www.packtpub.com/authors.

Customer support

Now that you are the proud owner of a Packt book, we have a number of things to help you to get the most from your purchase.

Downloading the example code

You can download the example code files for all Packt books you have purchased from your account at http://www.PacktPub.com. If you purchased this book elsewhere, you can visit http://www.PacktPub.com/support and register to have the files e-mailed directly to you.

Errata

Although we have taken every care to ensure the accuracy of our content, mistakes do happen. If you find a mistake in one of our books—maybe a mistake in the text or the code—we would be grateful if you would report this to us. By doing so, you can save other readers from frustration and help us improve subsequent versions of this book. If you find any errata, please report them by visiting http://www.packtpub.com/support, selecting your book, clicking on the **errata submission form** link, and entering the details of your errata. Once your errata are verified, your submission will be accepted and the errata will be uploaded on our website, or added to any list of existing errata, under the Errata section of that title. Any existing errata can be viewed by selecting your title from http://www.packtpub.com/support.

Piracy

Piracy of copyright material on the Internet is an ongoing problem across all media. At Packt, we take the protection of our copyright and licenses very seriously. If you come across any illegal copies of our works, in any form, on the Internet, please provide us with the location address or website name immediately so that we can pursue a remedy.

Please contact us at copyright@packtpub.com with a link to the suspected pirated material.

We appreciate your help in protecting our authors, and our ability to bring you valuable content.

Questions

You can contact us at questions@packtpub.com if you are having a problem with any aspect of the book, and we will do our best to address it.

FreeCAD [How-to]

Welcome to *FreeCAD [How-to]*. This book will provide an introduction to the organization and versatility of this open source application. The recipes described in this book will introduce most of the concepts used throughout FreeCAD so that knowledge gained in one area will help you explore the other areas more efficiently.

FreeCAD is a general purpose modeling tool aimed at the engineering world. Unlike other modeling tools such as Blender or Maya, which are designed for animators and artists, FreeCAD puts heavy emphasis on parametric, feature-based design of three dimensional solids.

A great deal of foresight and planning has gone into the underlying technology of FreeCAD. The result is a tool that is powerful, easy to use, and easy to extend with the powerful scripting language Python.

This first part of this book will help you get familiar with the FreeCAD interface and philosophy. We'll look at a couple of specific techniques for modeling objects. The later recipes will focus more on using Python to automate and extend FreeCAD.

Getting and installing FreeCAD (Must know)

This recipe will describe the options available for installing FreeCAD on the three major platforms (Windows, Mac, and Linux). It will briefly cover the steps for installation of a stable release version.

Getting ready

FreeCAD is still under heavy development. Stable releases are provided periodically that are tested and debugged. These releases will lack the most current features and may not match many of the recipes described in this book.

Detailed instructions are provided on the FreeCAD site for installation on all three platforms along with removal and troubleshooting information.

How to do it...

1. For most casual users, the stable version binaries are the best place to start learning FreeCAD.

2. Start by visiting the FreeCAD site at `http://free-cad.sourceforge.net/`.

3. The main page of the FreeCAD site has a panel with download links for the current stable release.

- ❏ For Windows, the stable release is provided as a 32-bit Microsoft Installer application (`.msi` file). Download the file to your computer and double-click it to run the installation program.

- ❏ The Linux (**Ubuntu**) link will direct you to a personal package archive (PPA). The packages here are for Ubuntu but should work on any recent Debian derived distribution. Both 32 and 64 bit versions are available through the PPA. Add the PPA to your repository manager and install it like any other application. FreeCAD is also available in the main Ubuntu repository, but this version is outdated and should be avoided.

- ❏ Mac OS X (Lion) is supported with a 64-bit installer package. The installer is distributed in a disk image. Download the disk image file. Mount it and run the *Install FreeCAD* package. In the past, Mac OS X packaging was supported by only a small team and packages were not always up to date. OS X users are encouraged to consider building from source.

There's more...

FreeCAD's development pace is very fast. New features and improvements are appearing almost daily in the unstable and development branches of the source code. After you've explored the basics, you may wish to explore features not yet available in the stable version. Let's look at some of the other installation options.

Daily builds

If you are using Linux and are willing to accept the risk of broken features and occasional crashes, you can install one of the daily builds. These are generated automatically by build scripts each day and consequently have had no formal testing. The daily build contains the most recent features and bug fixes committed to the source code by the developers.

Daily builds aren't available for Windows but an unstable binary installer is periodically built. Download it from `http://sourceforge.net/projects/free-cad/files/FreeCAD%20Windows/`.

Building from source

Detailed instructions for building FreeCAD from source is beyond the scope of a How-to book, but an overview of the major steps may help:

1. **Meet the prerequisites**: You'll need a compiler and all the dependency libraries. FreeCAD has a long list of dependencies and getting them all in place can be a chore. This is much easier on a Linux computer since most or all of the dependencies can be downloaded from the software manager.

    For Windows, the FreeCAD site also provides a *libpack* download to simplify the dependency requirements.

2. **Obtain the source code**: FreeCAD source is maintained in a Git repository available at `git://free-cad.git.sourceforge.net/gitroot/free-cad/free-cad`.

3. **Compiling**: The specifics steps for compiling vary from platform to platform but are generally simple once the source and dependencies are in place. Study the page for your platform on the FreeCAD site.

Third-party builds

The FreeCAD site also maintains a list of alternate builds. These are binary installations that are created and maintained by people and organizations outside the FreeCAD project. They may include custom features or may be optimized for specific operating systems. At the time of writing, there were third-party builds for OpenSuse, Fedora, Slackware, ArchLinux, Gentoo, and others.

Understanding the FreeCAD interface (Must know)

FreeCAD is designed to be flexible, extensible, and task oriented.

The core functionality is divided into **workbenches**. Each workbench gathers the most frequently used tools for a particular task. This recipe will guide you through the FreeCAD user interface and introduce some concepts that are common across all workbenches.

Getting ready

Launch FreeCAD and orient yourself with the screenshot and the names of the major parts of the interface. The images and examples in this book are from a 0.13 development snapshot.

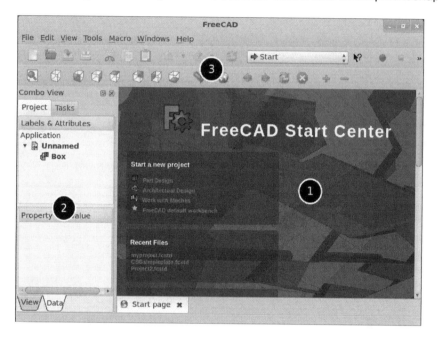

The default view is **Start page**—an embedded browser showing interesting video links, examples, and other news.

The user interface is divided into three main areas:

1. The 3D area allows you to see and navigate around your design in space.
2. The combo view shows a hierarchical view of the project or the state of the current task.
3. The tool bars and workbench switcher gives access to the various tools.

How to do it...

1. Open a new document by clicking on the menu **File | New**. The 3D view will switch to show an empty space. In the default orientation the camera position is looking down onto a plane defined by the X and Y axes. The Z axis is pointed directly at the camera. A coordinate indicator in the corner helps you orient yourself in the 3D space.

2. Click on the workbench switcher and select the **Part** workbench. Then click on the **Create a box solid** icon to insert a cube into the project.

3. You can have multiple projects open at the same time. You can also open multiple views of the same project. Open a second view of the project by clicking on the menu **View | Create new view**. You can switch views with the tabs below the 3D window or you can tile the views to have multiple perspectives at once. In this following screenshot, two projects are open, each with two views:

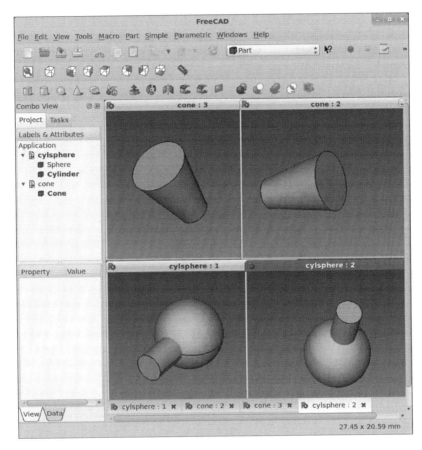

4. You can change the view of your project by **panning**, **rotating**, and **zooming**. Select objects by clicking on them to change their properties. The specific mouse and keyboard commands for doing this are called "navigation styles". FreeCAD supports four styles by default: *Inventor*, *CAD*, *Blender*, and *Touchpad*.

You can change the style used in the current view by right-clicking on the 3D canvas.

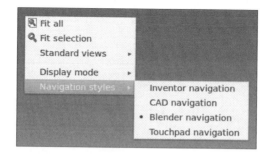

Changing the style through the **Edit | Preferences** menu will change the style for all views currently open and set the selection as the default for new views. The default style, **CAD navigation**, is unintuitive for some users since it requires clicking both the left and center mouse buttons at the same time to rotate. The **Mouse...** button in the **Display** preferences will show which button combinations perform each action.

5. Select the box and tap the space bar to toggle the object visibility property. Visibility is one of many properties of any object on screen. With the box still selected, examine the lower part of the combo-view. The properties of the selected object are shown on the two tabs (**View** and **Data**).

6. Click on the **Measure distance** icon, and then click two points on the box in the 3D window. A dimension will be shown and a distance object will be added to the tree.

7. You can select the distance object in the tree and explore its properties.

8. As the project complexity grows, you may need to perform an action on multiple objects at the same time. Select multiple objects by holding the *Ctrl* key while selecting with the mouse.

How it works...

The **View/Data** tabs reflect a deep design characteristic of FreeCAD. The data necessary to construct the object (size, type, placement, and rotation) is separated from the data needed to show it on screen (color, line style, visibility, and transparency).

Most operations in FreeCAD are non-destructive and result in new objects being added to the project tree. Each new object has its own **View** and **Data** tabs and preserves its relationship to its simple precursor. This makes it possible to delete the later objects and revert to the simpler object if needed.

As objects are added and modified, they are organized in the combo-view tree in a hierarchical way. Generally, the last child object is displayed and parent objects are hidden automatically.

There's more...

FreeCAD uses the term "view" to refer to several related concepts.

Default views

Eight default views are provided with icons in the tool bar to make it easy to position the project on the screen. These views are actually orientations of your work and shouldn't be confused with the view windows described previously.

The term view also refers to the camera projection type: *orthographic* or *perspective*.

Freezing and Saving views

You can preserve a favorite orientation of your work by freezing it (*Shift+F*). This adds a menu item for the frozen view to let you easily return to this orientation later.

Python and Report views

FreeCAD has two other important windows that are hidden by default and that are confusingly also called "views". The Python console will be discussed at length in the later sections of this book. The Report views provide useful information about what FreeCAD is doing behind the scenes.

CSG modeling in the Part workbench (Must know)

Constructive Solid Geometry (CSG) is a modeling technique that combines primitive solids with Boolean operations to create more complex shapes. FreeCAD's CSG tools are found on the **Part workbench.**

This recipe will use the Part workbench to model a simple part—an offset mounting bracket for a NEMA 17 stepping motor.

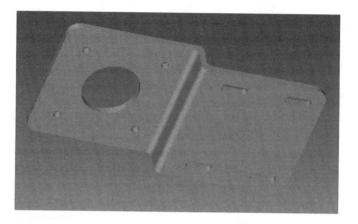

Getting ready

Create a new empty document and orient the view to the top using the **Set to top view** top-view icon or by pressing the number 2. Use the Workbench Changer to switch to the **Part** workbench.

How to do it...

1. Model the bent metal plate by adding and positioning three box solids. Add the first box to the drawing, and select its node in the project tree. Switch to the **Data** tab and edit the properties to make it 2.5 x 50 x 50 mm (height, length, width).

2. Create a second box with the same dimensions but edit the *placement* to move the box 50 mm in the X direction and 10 mm in the Z direction. This will place the second cube next to the first and shifted upward.

3. Add a third cube to connect them. Make its dimensions 10 x 2.5 x 50 mm and shift its placement 50 mm in the X direction.

4. If you rotate your view slightly, your three solids should look like the following figure:

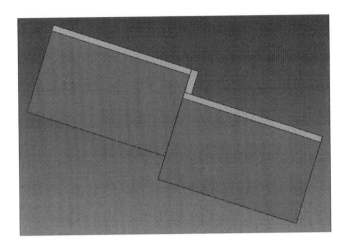

5. Next we'll create the slots. FreeCAD doesn't have a slot feature so we'll make a solid in the shape of the hole we want. Later, we'll subtract it from the plate to create the hole.

6. Add another box and set its dimensions to 10 x 10 x 3 mm.

7. We want the slot to have rounded ends so we will fillet the box. Select the box and press the menu **Part | Fillet**.

8. The combo view will switch to the **Tasks** panel and show the fillet options. You can use this to refine your edge selection and set the radius of the fillet. For our example, select **Edge1**, **Edge3**, **Edge5**, and **Edge7**. We used a value of 1 for the radius. Clicking on the **OK** button will apply the change. If you make a mistake, double-click the fillet object in the tree to change the properties and try again.

9. Once the cube looks right, select it and duplicate it with the menu item **Edit | Duplicate selection**. Repeat this twice more so that we have a total of four fillet objects. Select each one and change its placement properties to move it into position on the raised part of the plate. The position is up to you. Just make sure the fillet objects completely penetrate the plate.

10. Now add five cylinders for the holes. Change their placement and radius properties. The center hole is 22.5 mm and the small screw holes are 2.5 mm.

11. With all the solids added to the project, it should like the following image:

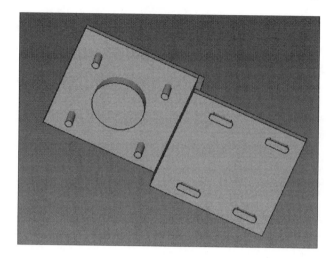

12. We're almost ready to subtract the cylinders and slots from our base plate, but we first need to clean things up a bit. In the project tree, select all of the cylinders and fillet objects. With all of them selected, click on the **Make a union of several shapes** icon:

13. Now select the three boxes for our base plate and repeat the operation, fusing them into a single object.

14. You should now have two fusion objects in the tree, one for the base plate and one for the holes that will be cut from it. First select the base plate fusion, and then with *Ctrl* held down, select the other. Click on the **Make a cut of two shapes** icon:

15. The order in which you select the objects is important. The first object will be cut by the second. If all goes well, you will have an object that looks almost like the image at the beginning of the recipe.

16. To finish it off, we've applied another round of fillets to the corners of the plate and to the corners of the bend. The complete object should look like the image at the beginning of this recipe.

How it works....

Union operations add objects together. The solids don't have to be touching or overlapping. After a union, they will have a single location and orientation.

A difference Boolean cuts the first object with the second. If the two objects don't overlap, the original object will be unaffected.

An intersection eliminates everything except the area where the original two objects overlapped.

After any of these operations, a new object is created and the original items become its hidden children. You can delete the parent node and toggle the original object visible to get back to where you were. Objects such as fillet and chamfer can be double-clicked to reopen the dialog that created them and adjust the options.

There's more...

There's often more than one way to do the same thing and the **Part** workbench has a few hidden extras.

Create primitives

FreeCAD can create many more primitive types than those in the toolbar. Use the **Create primitives** tool to create many other. For example, a spring-like parametric helix.

Why doesn't my part look right?

If your part doesn't look like the example at the beginning of this recipe, try playing with the **View** properties of the final object. Change the **Display Mode** to **shaded**.

Recording and editing a macro (Should know)

Macros are commands that represent a series of commands or key strokes and can take the drudgery out of repetitive tasks. Macro recording can be used to automate tasks that don't warrant full blown script programming. This recipe will cover the steps required to record, edit, and run a macro.

Getting ready

Locate the **Macro** toolbar or **Macro** menu item.

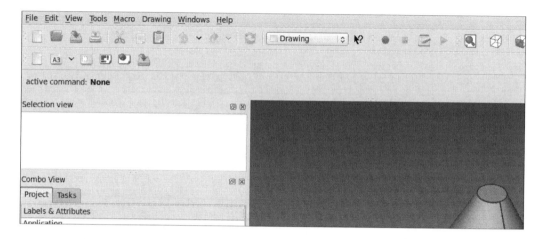

How to do it...

1. Press the red record button shown in the following screenshot:

2. The macro recording dialog box will pop up. Give your macro a name and save it:

3. Perform the tasks that you want recorded. You can create a macro of whatever you normally do in FreeCAD. Macros that deal with simple part creation are easiest to start with. Try creating a box in the **Part** workbench and change its width to 20 mm.

4. When you are done recording the tasks, press the green button to stop recording:

5. Run your macro by selecting the button that looks like a sketch pad:

6. Select the name of the macro that you created and click on **Execute**:

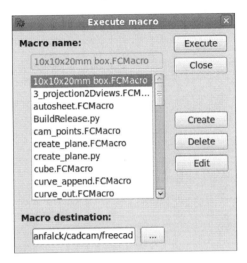

In FreeCAD, macros are just a step-by-step representation of the commands that are saved as a Python script, with a FreeCAD macro file extension *.FCMacro. As you perform tasks in FreeCAD, they have a corresponding Python command that is running in the background. A FreeCAD macro just captures those commands and saves them into a file that you can reuse.

If you have problems saving macros, it could be because of a setting in macro preferences for FreeCAD. Open general preferences by clicking on **Edit | Preferences | General** and then click on the **Macro** tab. Under **Macro recording settings** the **Macro path** should have a valid path to a file directory in it. If it doesn't, click on the button to the right of it and correct it with a valid directory name.

There's more...

Most FreeCAD commands can be accessed with macros and Python scripting.

Taking advantage of the power of macros

Macros actually record Python instructions as they are executed. We also have the ability to read and edit them later. Open our new macro with the **Edit** button in the macro dialog. This will open our macro in FreeCAD's built-in macro editor. The following is our code:

```
# Macro Begin: /home/freecad/10x10x20mm box.FCMacro ++
import FreeCAD
import Part


#Gui.activateWorkbench("PartWorkbench")
App.ActiveDocument.addObject("Part::Box","Box")
#App.ActiveDocument.recompute()
#Gui.SendMsgToActiveView("ViewFit")
FreeCAD.getDocument("Unnamed").getObject("Box").Width = 20.00


# Macro End: /home/freecad/10x10x20mm box.FCMacro ++
```

Downloading the example code

You can download the example code files for all Packt books you have purchased from your account at http://www.PacktPub.com. If you purchased this book elsewhere, you can visit http://www.PacktPub.com/support and register to have the files e-mailed directly to you.

The lines that begin with # are not executed by FreeCAD; they are Python comments. Comments help us understand what is happening in the code. The only lines of code that are actually executed are as follows:

```
import FreeCAD
import Part


App.ActiveDocument.addObject("Part::Box","Box")
FreeCAD.getDocument("Unnamed").getObject("Box").Width = 20.00
```

The statements that start with `import` open some major modules that are needed for our macro to be able to function. `import Part` lets us make geometric objects such as boxes, cylinders, spheres, and a lot more. `App.ActiveDocument.addObject("Part::Box","Box")` actually creates the box.

You can edit macros to do things that they didn't do originally, while they were being recorded. Open the macro in the built-in FreeCAD editor by pressing the button that looks like a text edit pad. Select your macro and then select the **Edit** button. You could change the values of parameters for many different objects. In our example macro, you could change the following two lines to have a different name and length:

```
App.ActiveDocument.addObject("Part::Box","newbox")
FreeCAD.getDocument("Unnamed").getObject("newbox").Width=20.5
```

Save your changes by selecting **File** | **Save** in the top menu. Then you can press the green playback icon to try out your altered macro:

Learn a bit of Python programming by reading macro scripts

Creating and editing macros is a good way of learning how to use Python within FreeCAD. Open your macros in the editor and play with them by changing different parameters and rerun them.

To learn more about the Python programming language, go to `http://docs.python.org/tutorial`.

Modeling a simple part with the Draft workbench (Must know)

Many 3D designs begin as two dimensional drawings that are extruded or rotated into the third dimension. For example, a two dimensional square can be extruded into a three dimensional cube. The **Draft** workbench provides tools for working with 2D geometry.

In this recipe, we'll draw and edit a 2D profile of a part. In a later recipe, we'll rotate this profile to create a 3D model of a timing pulley.

Getting ready

Start a new project and switch to the **Draft** workbench. Make sure your view is set to top.

Change your draft preferences to make it easier to snap to the grid. Set the **Grid spacing** value to 1.000 and the **Main lines every** value to 10. Set the **Snap range** to about 4px.

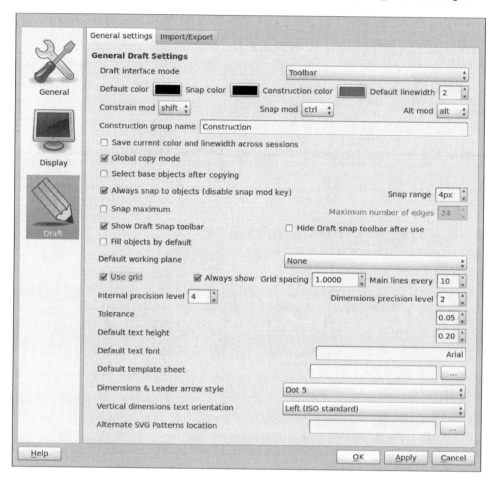

How to do it...

1. Select the wire tool. Deselect the **Relative** checkbox. Points of a wire can be added by clicking the canvas or manually by keying in coordinates. Manually enter the first point at X = 3.175, Y = -5, and Z = 0. You can *Tab* from field to field and hit *Enter* on Z to create the point.

2. Continue adding a second point at X = 3.175, Y = 10, Z = -0.

3. Enter the remaining points working clockwise around until your wire looks like the following image. The remaining points can be added by clicking the canvas, and snapping to the grid if you prefer. Holding the *Shift* key will force new segments to be orthogonal.

When you have entered the last point but before returning to the starting point, click on **Close** to automatically close the wire and exit the tool:

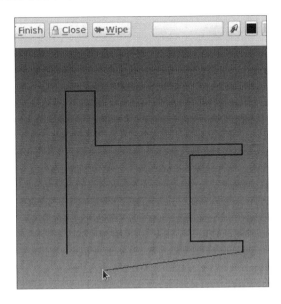

1. Before we can edit any part of the wire we have to explode it into a collection of edges. Select the wire in the project tree. Select the **Draft** menu and click on the **Downgrade** button three times.

2. We'll replace the square edge of the rim with a arc. Make sure that midpoint and endpoint are enabled on the snapping toolbar. Use the arc tool and draw a curve on the rim.

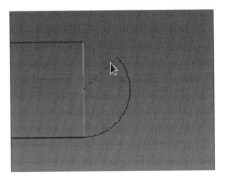

3. Repeat for the other rim, then delete the old straight edges.

4. Select all the edges in the tree. Select the **Draft** menu and click on the **Upgrade** button to rejoin them into a wire.

How it works...

Complex topological shapes are built up from more simple geometric objects such as lines, circles, and arcs. For example, an **edge** can be made from a line connecting two **vertices**, each of which is a just a point in space. An edge can also be an arc or a circle. When multiple edges are connected end-to-end they become a **wire**. A closed wire can be upgraded to a **face**, and if a collection of faces fully encloses a volume it is a **solid**. If a group of faces doesn't fully enclose the space (that is, one or more faces are missing) it is called a **shell**.

The **Draft** workbench provides tools for directly creating, modifying, and converting between these data types.

There's more....

In addition to the tools for creating and modifying 2D geometry, recent versions of the **Draft** workbench have a couple of powerful and useful features.

Create arrays

The array tool creates arrays of individual objects. Polar arrays are useful for creating bolt circles and gears. Ortho arrays create grid-like arrangements.

Select the object to be duplicated and click on the array tool. Then adjust the properties of the array in the **Data** tab. These include the number of copies, rotation center, and array type.

Converting drafts and sketches

A **sketch** is another way of drawing 2D data in FreeCAD, which we'll be looking at in more detail in a later recipe. Sketches and drafts serve different purposes but it's sometimes desirable to convert between them. The Draft workbench has a tool for doing this conversion. Be aware that sketch-specific data will be lost when it's converted to a draft.

Rotating and extruding to create parts (Should know)

2D drawings are converted into 3D models either by extruding them along an axis, or by rotating them around an axis.

Getting ready

Use the **Draft** workbench to draw a closed profile of a part. For our example, we're using the timing pulley profile from the *Modeling a simple part with the Draft workbench (Must know)* recipe.

How to do it...

1. Switch to the **Draft** workbench.

2. Select the wire and click on the **Upgrade** button to convert it to a face.

3. Switch to the **Part** workbench.

4. Press the **Revoke a selected shape** button:

5. In the **Revolve** dialog, select the shape to rotate.

6. Select the axis around which to revolve. For our example, use the Y axis. Leave the other settings unchanged and click on **OK**.

7. The revolved object is added to the project.

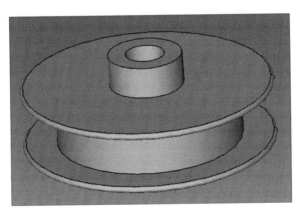

How it works...

FreeCAD has two kinds of wire objects. Draft wires, called **dwire** in later versions, have additional features and properties on the **Data** tab. The wire used in our example contains arcs and is a regular wire. If you were to rotate the wire without upgrading it to a face first, the result you would see on screen would look exactly the same. However, the object would be a hollow shell. This can cause problems if you do additional Boolean operations. By rotating a face instead of a wire, the area swept out by the rotation is a solid.

Extruding an object works similarly. A shape is selected and parameters are given for the direction and distance to extrude. Applying an extrusion to our original wire gives a very different result.

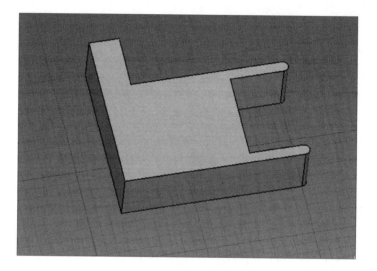

The extrude and rotate tools in the **Part** workbench can be used on many kinds of objects including sketches. The kind of object produced depends on the original object.

Input shape	Output shape
Vertex	Edge
Edge	Face
Wire (closed)	Shell
Dwire	Solid
Face	Solid
Shell	Compound Solid
Sketch	Shell

The Part Design workbench has its own tools for rotating and extruding (called **padding**) sketches to create parts. The Part Design pad and rotation tools can only be used on sketches. They always create solids if the sketch is closed and will fail otherwise.

There's more...

FreeCAD has another tool for turning 2D geometry into 3D objects.

Lofting

Two or more wires can be used to define the bounds of a solid and the loft tool will create a solid by sweeping the area between them. In the following screenshot, two rectangular shapes were positioned one above the other and rotated slightly. The loft tool creates a twisted cuboid by connecting the two:

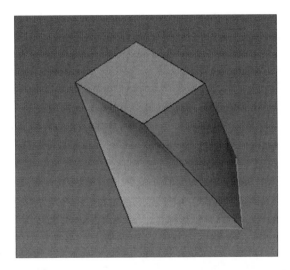

Creating 3D solids with Python (Become an expert)

Python is a high-level programming language that is easy to learn, easy to read, and powerful. To learn more about the Python programming language, go to www.python.org.

FreeCAD's use of Python as its scripting language makes it extremely flexible for modeling parts. With Python in control, a user can do things that would be hard to do manually.

With this recipe, a model of a servo motor is rendered.

Getting ready

For this recipe the Python console is needed. Make sure it's open. In the menu bar, click on **View | Views** and then make sure **Python console** is checked. The **Python console** will be located in the bottommost panel in FreeCAD. It looks similar to the following screenshot:

You will also need to have a document open in order for the Python scripted solid model to have a place to appear.

 Python is case sensitive. Make sure that you type in the following recipe exactly as it is shown. Python is also sensitive to indentation, so take care not to add extra spaces or tabs at the beginning of any line.

How to do it...

1. Enter the following text into the Python console:

```
import Part
from FreeCAD import Vector

plate = Part.makeBox(40,40,5,Vector(-20,-20,0))
hole1= Part.makeCylinder(1.5,5,Vector(-15,-15,0))
hole2= Part.makeCylinder(1.5,5,Vector(-15,15,0))
hole3= Part.makeCylinder(1.5,5,Vector(15,15,0))
hole4= Part.makeCylinder(1.5,5,Vector(15,-15,0))
faceplate = plate.cut(hole1)
faceplate = faceplate.cut(hole2)
faceplate = faceplate.cut(hole3)
faceplate = faceplate.cut(hole4)
motorbody=Part.makeCylinder(17.5,60,Vector(0,0,5))
shaft = Part.makeCylinder(3.175,15,Vector(0,0,-15))
servo = motorbody.fuse(faceplate)
```

```
servo = servo.fuse(shaft)
servo.translate(Vector(-20,-20,0))
servo.rotate(Vector(0,0,0),Vector(0,1,0),-90)
Part.show(servo)
```

2. Make sure to press the *Enter* key after the last line.

3. You should see a 3D solid in the graphics screen of FreeCAD that looks similar to the following graphic:

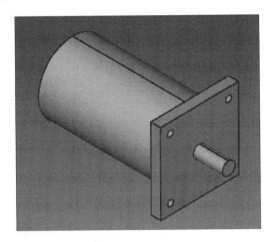

How it works...

At the start of the script, FreeCAD needs some of its modules imported:

```
import Part
from FreeCAD import Vector
```

Without importing these, the script could not do anything beyond what is already in the standard Python library. The Part module gives access to geometric objects in FreeCAD. The Vector module is related to translating and rotating objects.

In lines like `plate = Part.makeBox(40,40,5,Vector(-20,-20,0))` the Part module gives us a way of creating a solid box that is 40 mm x 40 mm x 5 mm big, which will be the face plate for our servo motor model. It is moved along a vector; 20 mm in the x direction; 20 mm in the y direction; and 0 mm in the z direction. FreeCAD allows us to create many types of solids in Python such as cylinders with `Part.makeCylinder`, spheres with `Part.makeSphere`, cones with `Part.makeCone`, and toruses with `Part.makeTorus`.

FreeCAD can cut 3D objects and fuse them to each other. In Python code that looks like this: `faceplate = plate.cut(hole1)`, we are cutting the plate with `hole1`. Fusing objects together can be seen in a line like `servo = motorbody.fuse(faceplate)`, where motor body is fused to faceplate.

At the end of the script, we make our servo motor visible by showing it using the following code:

```
Part.show(servo)
```

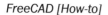
There's more...

You can use the Python console in FreeCAD to help you explore the depths of the the Part module. Just start typing `Part.` into the console and FreeCAD's auto-completion feature will show you what classes are available and give you tips. The `.` is what causes the console to auto complete.

Here is what the auto completion feature looks like in action:

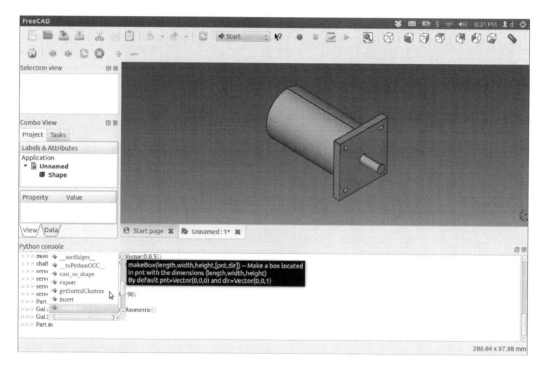

Notice how it gives you a helpful tip on the `makeBox` class.

Learn more about part scripting online

Go to `https://sourceforge.net/apps/mediawiki/free-cad/index.php?title=Topological_data_scripting` for more info and examples of how to work with Python in FreeCAD. More examples can also be found by searching `http://www.thingiverse.com/` with the keyword `freecad`.

Creating a custom dialog to automate a task (Become an expert)

The Python programming language in FreeCAD allows us to use PyQt4 or PySide to add our own widgets to make custom graphical user interfaces. In this recipe, we will create a dialog box that lets us create a simple box.

Getting ready

If the **Draft** workbench is functioning properly in FreeCAD, then you already have PyQt4 installed on your computer. Open a new document, so that we have space for our 3D box to appear.

How to do it...

The following is some code that will make a dialog pop-up, which lets us create a 3D solid box with a few parameters:

1. Type the following code into the Python console exactly as shown. Python is case and indent sensitive. Be consistent on indentation. We will use four spaces per indent here. An intent looks like a tab in this text. I have added \ (backslashes) to some lines that won't fit on the printed page in their complete form.

```python
from PyQt4 import QtGui,QtCore
import Part,FreeCAD
from FreeCAD import Base,Vector

class BoxExample(QtGui.QWidget):
    def __init__(self):
        super(BoxExample, self).__init__()
        self.initUI()
    def initUI(self):
        self.setGeometry(100, 100,300, 200)
        self.setWindowTitle('Make a Box!')
        self.lengthLabel = QtGui.QLabel("Length: ",self)
        self.lengthLabel.move(50, 15)
        self.length = QtGui.QLineEdit(self)
        self.length.move(100, 15)
        self.widthLabel = QtGui.QLabel("Width: ",self)
        self.widthLabel.move(50, 50)
        self.width = QtGui.QLineEdit(self)
        self.width.move(100, 50)
        self.heightLabel = QtGui.QLabel("Height: ",self)
        self.heightLabel.move(50, 85)
```

```
        self.height = QtGui.QLineEdit(self)
        self.height.move(100, 85)
        self.centered=QtGui.QCheckBox("Center on XY",self)
        self.centered.move(80, 115)
        self.centerbox = False
        self.centered.stateChanged.connect(self.changeState)
        self.okButton = QtGui.QPushButton("Create Box",self)
        self.okButton.move(160, 150)
        self.show()
        QtCore.QObject.connect \
    (self.okButton, QtCore.SIGNAL("pressed()"),self.box)
    def changeState(self, state):
        console=FreeCAD.Console
        if state == QtCore.Qt.Checked:
            console.PrintMessage("Box will be centered\n")
            self.centerbox = True
        else:
            self.centerbox = False
    def box(self):
        l = float(self.length.text())
        w = float(self.width.text())
        h = float(self.height.text())
        if self.centerbox == True:
            box = Part.makeBox(l,w,h)
            box.translate(Base.Vector(-l/2,-w/2,0))
        else:
            box = Part.makeBox(l,w,h)
        Part.show(box)

d = BoxExample()
```

2. Press the *Enter* key twice after typing in the last line.

3. When the dialog box pops up, fill in the values and click on the **Create Box** button. A simple 3D box should appear in the FreeCAD document. It looks similar to the following screenshot:

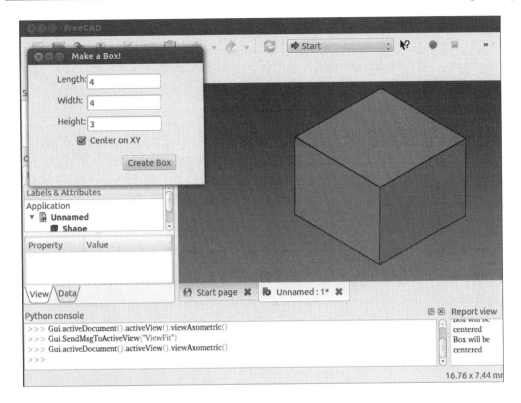

How it works...

We start by creating a class that holds all of our dialog box functions:

```
class BoxExample(QtGui.QWidget):
```

The code within the BoxExample class that is part of the function def initUI(self):
is used to set up the widgets for our dialog. Lines that have QtGui.QLabel in them let us
label the textboxes that are made with QtGui.QLineEdit(self). There is a checkbox and
a button towards the end of the function in the form of QtGui.QCheckBox and QtGui.
QPushButton respectively. def changeState(self, state): is used to see if our
Center on XY checkbox is checked.

The following lines of code are used to connect the button labeled **Create Box** to the
next function:

```
QtCore.QObject.connect \
(self.okButton, QtCore.SIGNAL("pressed()"),self.box)
```

I used the \ continuation character to fit one long line of code onto the formatted text of this book, so these two lines appear to be one to Python.

The `def box(self)` function does the work to create the 3D solid box in the document. `box = Part.makeBox(l,w,h)` creates the box and `Part.show(box)` makes it appear in our document.

Within FreeCAD Python scripting, we don't use a main call, like we would have if we were making a standalone application. Instead we use `d = BoxExample()` to invoke and show our `BoxExample()` class. This is what turns our dialog box on.

There's more...

To learn more about dialog creation for FreeCAD go to `https://sourceforge.net/apps/mediawiki/free-cad/index.php?title=Dialog_creation`.

Learn more about Python and PyQt programming

One of the first places that a new Python programmer should check out is the official Python documentation website available at `http://python.org/doc/`.

There is also a good intro to PyQt programming available at `http://zetcode.com/tutorials/pyqt4/firstprograms/`.

Make things easier by using Qt Designer

To make programming dialogs a lot easier, you will want to use Qt Designer, a graphical dialog creation tool. It will let you create dialogs with a graphical editor that can be converted into Python code. If you are using Ubuntu Linux as your operating system, look in Synaptic for **qtdesigner**.

This following web page gives a good introduction to creating dialogs for FreeCAD:

`https://sourceforge.net/apps/mediawiki/free-cad/index.php?title=Dialog_creation`

Modeling with constraints (Must know)

Many of the tools in the Part Design workbench will seem familiar from the Draft workbench. The workflow however is quite different. Built around the idea of feature-based design, geometry in the Part Design sketcher is first drawn very roughly and then refined with constraints. As the constraints are added, the built-in solver will adjust the geometry to satisfy the constraint requirements.

In this recipe, we'll design a simple part that has features in two axes and show how it can be revised with constraints. In a later recipe, we'll add features to this part.

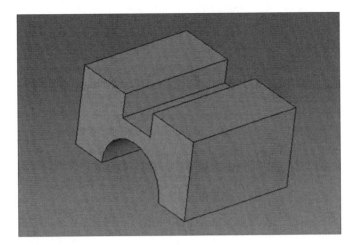

Getting ready

Begin with a new, empty document. Switch to the **Part Design** workbench and click on the button to create a new or edit the selected sketch. A dialog will popup asking which plane you want the sketch oriented on. Select the **XZ-Plane** option and click on **OK**.

How to do it...

1. Roughly draw the end profile of the part. Don't worry about accuracy at this point. The following example was drawn with an arc and a wire:

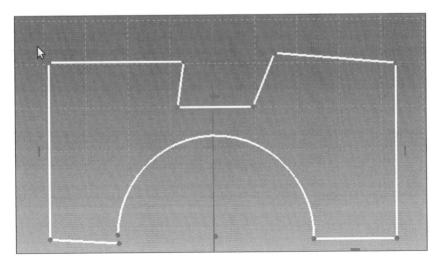

2. Add geometric constraints. Constraints are added by selecting the parts of the sketch to be constrained and pressing the appropriate constraint button. A new constraint icon will be added to the drawing and it will be listed in the left-side panel.

3. Start by adding horizontal and vertical constraints to any crooked lines.

   If lines are supposed to connect, select the vertexes and add coincident constraints.

   Select pairs of matching lines and add an equality constraint. This forces the lines to be equal length.

4. When the sketch looks symmetrical, add dimension constraints. Start by constraining the most important dimensions. For instance, we've constrained the radius of the arc to 25 mm.

5. As you add constraints, watch the solver message at the top of the task panel. As the number of Degrees Of Freedom (DOF) approaches zero you may find it difficult to add constraints without getting a conflicting constraints error. Grabbing a vertex or segment and dragging it can show you where the sketch is still under constrained.

6. If the sketch gets to 2 DOF and dragging a segment just moves the entire sketch, it's time to lock it. Pick a vertex (we used the center of the arc) and click on the lock button. This will add vertical and horizontal distance constraints which lock the vertex to the origin of the coordinate system. A fully constrained sketch will turn green. Celebrate.

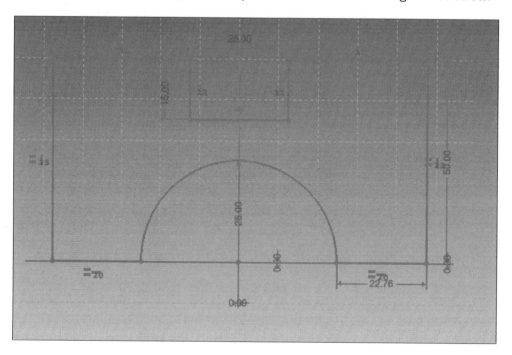

7. Click on the **close** button in the task panel. Use the pad tool to pad the sketch to 75 mm and rotate the sketch to see your part.

8. Even after the sketch has been padded, you can still edit it by double-clicking it in the tree. When saved, your changes will be immediately incorporated into the part.

How it works...

Constraints limit the ways in which an object can transform. A circle on a plane can be moved in two directions and can have its radius changed. Thus it has three degrees of freedom. When its radius is constrained it has 2 DOF and when its center is locked in X and Y, it is considered fully constrained.

Geometric constraints are those that affect the shape or relationship of entities; horizontal, vertical, tangent, symmetric, and so on.

Dimension constraints have a number. Double-click the constraint to edit the value. Length, radius, and angle are all dimension constraints.

Modeling with constraints is very practical for discrete parts where the features have an implied relationship between them.

There's more...

Avoiding and eliminating conflicting constraints is the biggest challenge most users face with the sketcher. Practice goes a long way towards improving your skills but following some basic guidelines will also help.

Apply constraints carefully

Apply symmetry constraints first. Next apply geometric constraints (horizontal, vertical, tangent, and so on) before dimension constraints (anything with a number).

When possible, fix the horizontal or vertical distance rather than constraining the length.

Try to apply coordinate locks last. In other words, try to get the sketch constrained with itself before you try to constrain it to the coordinate system.

Use multiple simple sketches

It's generally easier to use several simple sketches to build up the complexity of your part rather than one large sketch with many constraints. Keep your sketches as simple as possible. Whenever possible, use chamfer and fillet operations on the solid rather than modeling the beveled or rounded corners in the sketch.

Using external constraints (Should know)

It's rare that all the features of the part we want to design are in the same two-dimensional plane.

Imagine that we want to add holes to the top surface of the part we designed in the *Modeling with constraints (Must know)* recipe as shown in the following screenshot. To do this, we need a way to associate a new sketch with the top face of the part.

An external constraint gives us a way to relate elements of our sketch to entities that are not in the sketch itself, like the face of a part.

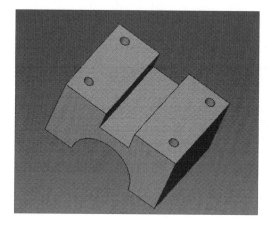

In this recipe we'll also show how features in a sketch can be related to an existing object.

Along the way, we'll also introduce construction lines and external constraints.

Getting ready

This recipe uses functionality from FreeCAD version 0.13 and later. Make sure you are using a recent release or development snapshot.

Open the model created in the *Modeling with constraints (Must know)* recipe. Set the view to **top** so you're looking down on the part from above.

How to do it...

1. Select the top face of the part so it is highlighted and click on the sketch button. The new sketch will be mapped to the face.

2. Draw four circles to represent our bolt holes. Select all four by clicking the edge (not the center) and set an equality constraint so they're the same size.

3. Select one of the four and add a radius constraint. Set the radius to 3.5 mm. Now all four can be resized by changing one number.

4. We want the holes to be positioned symmetrically. Select the centers of the top two holes and the vertical axis. Add a symmetry constraint. Repeat for the bottom two holes. The two sets of circles are now independently symmetrical.

5. Draw a line from the center of the top-right hole to the center of the bottom-right hole. Make sure the end points are coincident with the center of each circle. Select the line and make it into a construction line by clicking on the construction mode icon.

6. Set a length constraint on the construction line of 50 mm.

7. Now we need a way to set the position of the holes relative to the edge of the part.

8. Click on the **External Constraint** icon and select the right edge of the original solid. The edge and its vertexes can now be referenced in constraints as though they were a part of the sketch.

9. Select the center of the bottom-right circle and the bottom-end point of the external constraint line. Add a horizontal distance constraint (11 mm). Repeat and add a vertical distance constraint (15 mm).

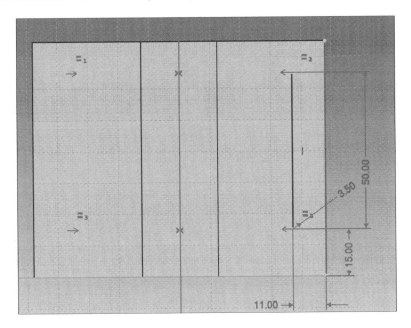

10. The sketch should be fully constrained. To create holes all the way through the block, close the sketch and use the pocket tool. Set the pocket depth to at least 50 mm.

How it works...

Sketches can be drawn on the planar faces of existing solids to add features such as protrusions or recesses.

Construction geometry can be added to any sketch. These lines, circles, and arcs don't become part of the final object but can take all the same constraints. They assist in drawing other entities and establishing relationships between entities.

An external constraint line is similar to a construction line but is an edge selected from the face on which a sketch is being drawn.

There's more...

To use external constraints, a sketch must be mapped to a face. This happens automatically when you begin a sketch by selecting a face of an object. However, it is also possible to apply an existing sketch to a face on which it wasn't originally drawn.

Mapping a sketch to a face

Select a face and click the menu **Part Design | Map Sketch** to face.

In the dialog, select which sketch to map to the face and click on **OK**. Mapping a sketch to the face puts the sketch into edit mode. Adjust the sketch if necessary and close it. A sketch can be remapped to a different face but cannot be mapped to multiple faces at the same time.

Adding or modifying constraints with Python (Become an expert)

In addition to using the Sketcher interactively and graphically we can use Python to program it automatically.

Getting ready

For this recipe, we need the Python console open. In the menu bar, open **View**, then **Views**, and then make sure that **Python console** is checked.

How to do it...

1. Enter the following code block into the console:

```
from Sketcher import *
import Part
import FreeCAD as App
from FreeCAD import Vector
if(App.activeDocument() == None):App.newDocument()

f = App.activeDocument().addObject("Sketcher::SketchObject",\
"Sketch")
f.addGeometry(Part.Line(Vector(0,0,0),Vector(2,20,0)))
f.addGeometry(Part.Line(Vector(0,0,0),Vector(20,2,0)))
f.Constraints = [Constraint('Vertical',0),\
Constraint('Horizontal',1)]
App.activeDocument().recompute()
```

2. Double-click on the **Sketch** icon in the Project tree.

3. Notice the horizontal and vertical constraint symbols (the small red bars). Also notice that the lines have end points but they aren't constrained.

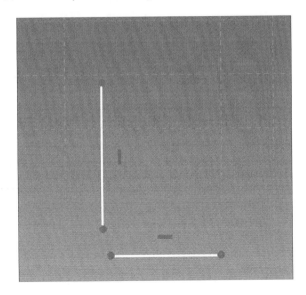

4. Grab either of the lines and move it and the other one won't move with it.

5. Add some more Python code to the console to constrain some points:

```
StartPoint = 1 ;
l = f.Constraints
l.append(Constraint('Coincident',0,StartPoint,1,StartPoint))
f.Constraints = l
App.activeDocument().recompute()
```

6. Notice how one end of each line has connected to the other.

7. Try moving one of the lines around the screen and you will see that the lines move together.

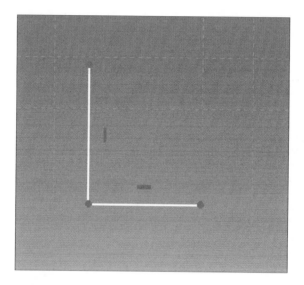

How it works...

1. Import all available functions in the Sketcher module:

    ```
    from Sketcher import *
    ```

2. We will need the Part module to make geometric objects:

    ```
    import Part
    ```

3. The FreeCAD module will let us manipulate the document:

    ```
    import FreeCAD as App
    ```

4. We will need to give our line segments end points, so we need:

    ```
    from FreeCAD import Vector
    ```

5. If a document isn't already open create a new one:

    ```
    if(App.activeDocument() == None): App.newDocument()
    ```

6. Create a new Sketch object:

```
f = App.activeDocument().addObject("Sketcher::SketchObject",\
"Sketch")
```

7. Add geometry to the sketch:

```
f.addGeometry(Part.Line(Vector(0,0,0),Vector(2,20,0)))
f.addGeometry(Part.Line(Vector(0,0,0),Vector(20,2,0)))
```

8. Add some constraints to the sketch to make the lines horizontal and vertical:

```
f.Constraints = [Constraint('Vertical',0),\
Constraint('Horizontal',1)]
```

9. Recompute the sketch to see things after changes:

```
App.activeDocument().recompute()
```

10. Let's add a name for startpoints on our lines:

```
StartPoint = 1
```

11. Create a proxy object that is equal to our original, because we cannot add constraints directly to it:

```
l = f.Constraints
```

12. Append more constraints to our proxy object. 0 is the first line and 1 is the second:

```
l.append(Constraint('Coincident',0,StartPoint,1,StartPoint))
```

13. Make the original constraints equal to the proxy and recompute:

```
f.Constraints = l
App.activeDocument().recompute()
```

There's more...

You can constrain your geometry with dimensions, using Python.

Add a length constraint to a line

You can add a length constraint to our second line as follows:

```
l.append((Constraint('DistanceX',1,20.0)))
```

Creating a drawing of a part (Should know)

The Drawing workbench lets us create 2D views of 3D objects for presentation in formats that are ideal for printing. In this recipe, we will create a drawing with three views.

Getting ready

Select a 3D object in a document and open the **Drawing** workbench:

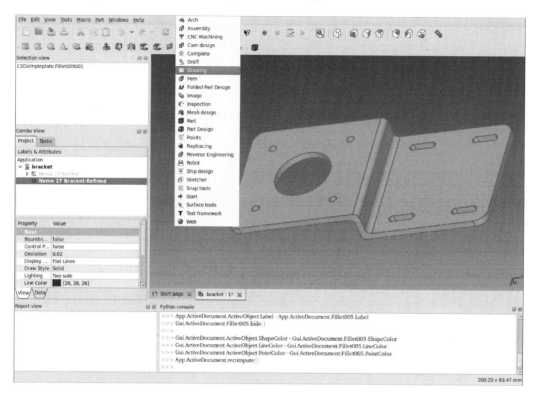

How to do it...

1. Select the **Insert new drawing** icon:

2. Pick the *Insert an orthographic projection* icon:

3. A new task will pop up in the **Task** panel. Select a **Primary View**:

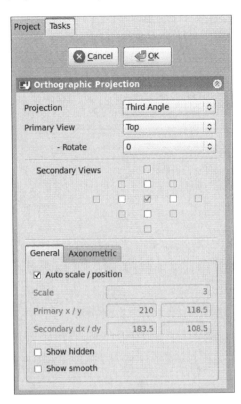

4. Select **Secondary Views**:

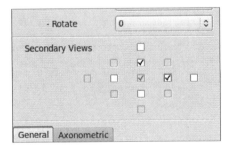

5. Click on the **OK** button in the **Task** panel.
6. While the **Page** icon is selected in the Project tree, click on its **Data** tab.

7. Double-click on the button that has **...** as its label.

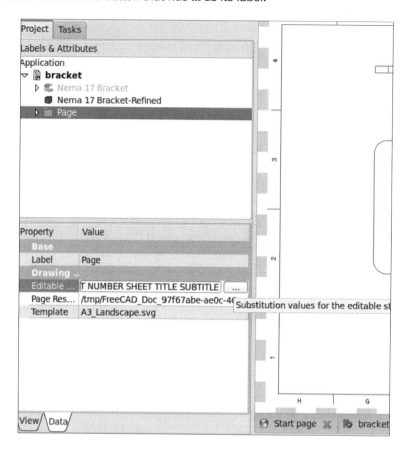

8. A text dialog box will popup. Edit the values, putting in your name, the date, and so on:

9. Click on the recompute button to see the results:

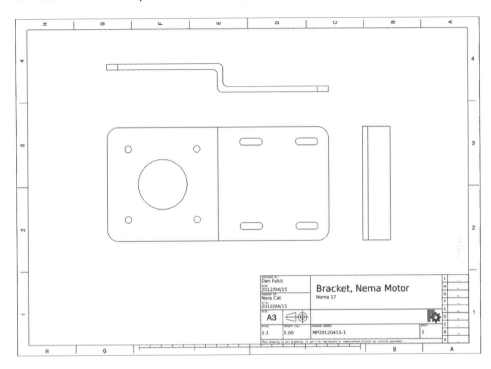

How it works...

FreeCAD uses algorithms from the OpenCascade CAD kernel to calculate 2D projections from 3D objects. FreeCAD takes advantage of this and inserts those projections onto a SVG canvas. This canvas is actually a template that was imported during step 1.

The Orthographic Projection dialog in the Task panel creates different projections at set angles, scales them, and spaces them in a consistent way.

The text dialog helps us edit SVG editable texts and fills in the text information in the bottom-right corner of the title block.

There's more...

If you want to give your drawing to someone who doesn't have FreeCAD, you might want to export it as a PDF file.

Export a PDF file from your drawing

Select the **Page** object in the Project tree. From the top menu, select **File** and then **Export PDF**. Give your file a name with a `*.pdf` extension and select a directory to save it to.

Exporting DXF files for other applications (Should know)

Most CAD applications don't live in a vacuum and need to be able to save to different file formats for other CADCAM programs to use. FreeCAD is no exception. There are some tasks that FreeCAD doesn't do especially well, such as dimensioning drawings. Other applications, such as LibreCAD or DraftSight do better in this area. Exporting 2D geometry to DXF format is an excellent way of facilitating this.

Getting ready

The first rule of exporting geometry is to make sure your geometry is clean and consistent. This means that the end points of lines and arcs that are meant to be connected should be connected with no gaps. Line segments hiding under other line segments should be deleted. Arcs and lines that are impossibly small should also be deleted. Don't leave any extra entities that aren't necessary in your document for exporting. 3D geometry does not export as DXF format in FreeCAD.

How to do it...

1. In the Project tree, select **2D geometry** from a **Sketch** or the **Draft** workbench. Be sure and select all geometry that you want exported.
2. From the top menu, select **File** and then **Export**.
3. In the lower-right corner of the **Export** file dialog, select **Autodesk DXF**.
4. In the **Name** entry box, give your file a name with the `*.dxf` extension.
5. Select the directory where you want your file saved.

How it works...

FreeCAD normally uses scripts from the **Draft** workbench to export 2D geometry.

Importing data (Should know)

Sometimes it is desirable to use geometry that was created in other CAD or modeling programs. FreeCAD can import a wide variety of file types. DXF, STEP, STL, SVG, VRML, Collada, and IDF are just some of the file formats that it can use.

In this recipe, we will open a DXF file and use the geometry in it to form a 3D solid.

Getting ready

You should have a DXF file produced by a CAD program such as QCAD, LibreCAD, Draftsight, or AutoCAD available to produce a DXF file.

1. In FreeCAD, open the **Draft** workbench and then select **Preferences** from the **Edit** menu.
2. In the **Preferences** dialog, click on the **Draft** icon and then click on the **Import/Export** tab.
3. Under **DXF format options**, change **Import style** to **None (fastest)**.
4. Uncheck all the other boxes in that same section. Click on **Apply** and then **OK**.

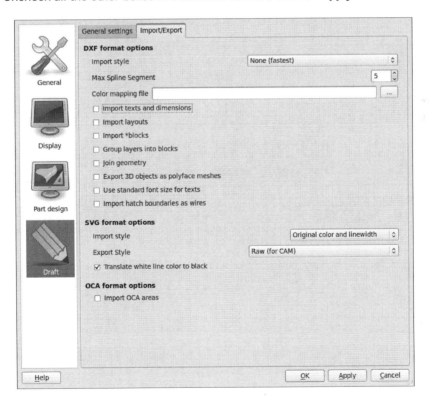

Create some geometry in another CAD program. For this example, we will use DraftSight to create a simple shape. The following is a polyline rectangle with four fillets and a circle:

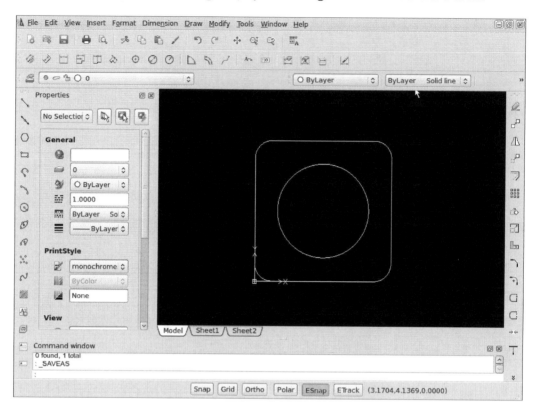

The lines and arcs in this drawing are a polyline. These will translate nicely into FreeCAD and help us create a solid to subtract the circle from.

Save the file as an ASCII type `dxf` (don't save as Binary).

How to do it...

1. In FreeCAD, select **Import** from the **File** menu.
2. Select the `dxf` file that you want to import.
3. In the **Combo View**, look at the **Project** tab and expand the icons.

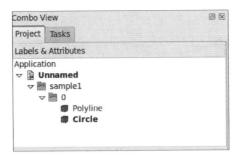

4. Switch to the **Draft** workbench so that we can **Upgrade** the Circle with the icon that looks like an arrow pointing upward.

5. Select the geometry labeled as **Polyline** and use the **Part** workbench with the **Extrude** icon to extrude it into a solid.

6. Extrude the geometry labeled **Circle** into a solid. Make sure that its height is the same as the solid made from Polyline.

7. Select the solid that you created from **Polyline** and then the solid created by **Circle**.

8. Use the **Boolean Cut** operation in **Part** workbench to subtract the **Circle** solid from the **Polyline** solid.

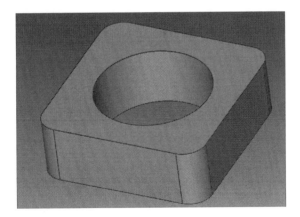

How it works...

DXF importing relies on code within the Draft workbench, so its settings are controlled from Draft preferences. The dxf polyline imported in as a face that could be extruded in the Part workbench. The Draft workbench has tools for changing other 2D geometry into faces, using the Upgrade tool, which allows the Part workbench to make solids from them. Faces will extrude as solids, whereas a closed shape without a face will just extrude into a thin object that looks like walls.

Index

Thank you for buying
FreeCAD [How-to]

About Packt Publishing

Packt, pronounced 'packed', published its first book "*Mastering phpMyAdmin for Effective MySQL Management*" in April 2004 and subsequently continued to specialize in publishing highly focused books on specific technologies and solutions.

Our books and publications share the experiences of your fellow IT professionals in adapting and customizing today's systems, applications, and frameworks. Our solution based books give you the knowledge and power to customize the software and technologies you're using to get the job done. Packt books are more specific and less general than the IT books you have seen in the past. Our unique business model allows us to bring you more focused information, giving you more of what you need to know, and less of what you don't.

Packt is a modern, yet unique publishing company, which focuses on producing quality, cutting-edge books for communities of developers, administrators, and newbies alike. For more information, please visit our website: www.packtpub.com.

About Packt Open Source

In 2010, Packt launched two new brands, Packt Open Source and Packt Enterprise, in order to continue its focus on specialization. This book is part of the Packt Open Source brand, home to books published on software built around Open Source licences, and offering information to anybody from advanced developers to budding web designers. The Open Source brand also runs Packt's Open Source Royalty Scheme, by which Packt gives a royalty to each Open Source project about whose software a book is sold.

Writing for Packt

We welcome all inquiries from people who are interested in authoring. Book proposals should be sent to author@packtpub.com. If your book idea is still at an early stage and you would like to discuss it first before writing a formal book proposal, contact us; one of our commissioning editors will get in touch with you.

We're not just looking for published authors; if you have strong technical skills but no writing experience, our experienced editors can help you develop a writing career, or simply get some additional reward for your expertise.

Ext JS 4 Web Application Development Cookbook

ISBN: 978-1-84951-686-0   Paperback: 488 pages

Over 110 easy-to-follow recipes backed up with real-life examples, walking you through basic Ext JS features to advanced application design using Sencha's Ext JS

1. Learn how to build Rich Internet Applications with the latest version of the Ext JS framework in a cookbook style

2. From creating forms to theming your interface, you will learn the building blocks for developing the perfect web application

3. Easy to follow recipes step through practical and detailed examples which are all fully backed up with code, illustrations, and tips

Sencha Touch Mobile JavaScript Framework

ISBN: 978-1-84951-510-8   Paperback: 316 pages

Build web applications for Apple iOS and Google Android touchscreen devices with this first HTML5 mobile framework

1. Learn to develop web applications that look and feel native on Apple iOS and Google Android touchscreen devices using Sencha Touch through examples

2. Design resolution-independent and graphical representations like buttons, icons, and tabs of unparalleled flexibility

3. Add custom events like tap, double tap, swipe, tap and hold, pinch, and rotate

Please check **www.PacktPub.com** for information on our titles

21914926R00040

Made in the USA
San Bernardino, CA
11 June 2015